THE BRC

A History from Beginning to End

BY HOURLY HISTORY

Copyright © 2024 by Hourly History.

All rights reserved.

The cover photo is a derivative of "Petroglypgh Group Nordic Bronze Age" (https://commons.wikimedia.org/wiki/File:Petroglypgh_Group_Nordic_Bronze_Age_007.svg) by Dillan Stradlin, used under CC BY-SA 4.0 (https://creativecommons.org/licenses/by-sa/4.0/deed.en)

Table of Contents

Introduction
The Fertile Crescent
Ancient Sumer
The Mediterranean
Central Asia and China
Central and Western Europe
The Nordic Bronze Age
International Trade and Globalization
Life in the Bronze Age
The Abrupt End of the Bronze Age
After the Bronze Age
Conclusion
Bibliography

Introduction

The notion of classifying the past in terms of ages is not new. As long ago as 700 BCE, the Greek poet Hesiod claimed that there had been five successive Ages of Man: Golden, Silver, Bronze, Heroic, and Iron. In the early nineteenth century, modern archeology began to adopt a similar concept.

Christian Jürgensen Thomsen was a respected Danish antiquarian, and in 1816, he was appointed as the head of antiquarian collections at the Museum of Northern Antiquities in Copenhagen (later to become the National Museum of Denmark). Thomsen set out displays of artifacts in the museum in chronological order, which led him to notice three distinct stages in early human history. The oldest artifacts, covering the vast majority of human history, were made from stone. After that, artifacts appeared that were made of metal, first using copper and then the harder and more durable bronze, an alloy made from copper and tin. After around two thousand years, bronze was replaced by iron as the main material used for making tools and weapons. This led Thomsen to propose a new way of classifying the periods of prehistory as the Stone, Bronze, and Iron Ages.

Thomsen's terminology was rapidly adopted by archeologists around the world and had, by the mid-nineteenth century, become widespread. Soon, this basic system was refined, with additional subdivisions being introduced. The Stone Age was subdivided into the Paleolithic (Old Stone Age), Mesolithic (Middle Stone Age), and Neolithic (New Stone Age). Some archeologists proposed adding a new transitional age, the Copper Age (also known as the Chalcolithic), between the Neolithic and the Bronze Age, though this wasn't widely adopted. The Bronze Age itself was subdivided into three periods—the Early, Intermediate, and Late—and it was generally accepted that these spanned a period beginning around 3300 BCE and ending around 1200 BCE.

Adopting these classifications was useful because it helped archeologists place new discoveries within an existing and widely understood context to make sense of them. The biggest problem with this system, however, is that it implies an orderly progression of technical development, and that isn't reflected in what we know of this period. Human history is rarely neatly divided into clear steps. New ideas emerge, and if they prove to be useful, they are shared and will spread intermittently and seemingly at random.

That was what appears to have happened during the Bronze Age. There wasn't a single moment when the world dropped its stone tools and began to use bronze replacements. Instead, this was a time of almost continual change, with different areas experiencing their own Bronze Age at quite different times. One of the few things that we can be fairly certain of is where bronze-working and the other changes that accompanied it began: in an area of the Middle East that would become known to archeologists as the Fertile Crescent.

Chapter One

The Fertile Crescent

"Bronze is the mirror of form, wine of the heart."

—Aeschylus

In the early twentieth century, American archeologist James Henry Breasted coined the phrase "Fertile Crescent" to describe one of the most important areas in early human development. This region, which includes present-day Jordan, Israel, Lebanon, Palestine, and Syria as well as parts of Kuwait, Turkey, and Iran, produced evidence of human settlements that, for the first time, appeared to use agriculture rather than hunting and gathering as the main source of food. It's difficult to over-emphasize the significance of this change.

Hunter-gatherers are, of necessity, nomadic. They move to follow game animals and the availability of naturally growing fruits and nuts. Their homes are temporary and portable, and they almost always live in small family groups rarely exceeding a few dozen people. This form of food acquisition is uncertain, and providing enough food for the whole group all year round means that everyone must be involved in hunting or gathering. There are no people who have the time to become artisans who will advance technology by exploring new and improved means of tool or weapon production for the simple reason that no one can be spared to do such work. For tens of thousands of years, human societies consisted solely of such small groups, and technology and science advanced hardly at all.

In the Fertile Crescent, for the first time, people began to switch to using agriculture as a means of replacing, or at least supplementing, hunting and gathering. This shift started somewhere around 10,000 BCE, and it took the form of clearing natural vegetation and replacing it with annual crops such as barley, flax, peas, chickpeas, and lentils. The fertile soil of this region, its predictable and stable climate, and its many rivers made it an ideal location for the first experimentation with agriculture.

The people of the Fertile Crescent also began to domesticate animals for the first time at around the same time—archeological evidence suggests that they may have kept cattle, pigs, sheep, and goats. This change had a major impact on almost every form of human activity. These people were no longer forced to be nomadic—they remained in the same place in order to produce crops and raise animals. Their homes were, for the first time, permanent structures.

Agriculture is a far more effective means of producing food than hunting and gathering, and for the first time, not every person in every group had to be constantly involved in the search for food. That meant that humans were living in permanent towns that included specialists who had the time to devote to producing improved metalwork and other crafts. Soon, agriculture would be enhanced by the development of new approaches that included irrigation, using the many rivers in the region to make even larger areas of land suitable for agriculture and to provide grazing for domesticated animals.

The Fertile Crescent helped to set the scene for what was to follow: the first human cities, the emergence of the first scientists, the first writing, and perhaps most important of all, the discovery that it was possible to use metal to produce tools and weapons that were much more effective than the stone implements that had gone before. By around 3500 BCE, developments in the Fertile Cresent meant that the world was poised on the brink of changes that would help shape the world in which we live today.

Chapter Two

Ancient Sumer

"A troubled mind makes you sick."

—Sumerian proverb

The Sumerians were one of the most mysterious of all ancient people. We simply don't know where they originated before they settled in a part of the Fertile Crescent that became known as Mesopotamia. We do know that these people were among the very first to make the transition into bronze-working. They also pioneered new forms of irrigation that transformed agriculture in the region, built the first cities, created the very first codes of law, produced scientists who investigated astronomy (among other things), and produced the first writing and even the first literature. It can be argued that the whole Bronze Age began with the Sumerians.

Around 3300 BCE, the Sumerians arrived at the Tigris and Euphrates Rivers in an area that would later become known as Mesopotamia (this word is derived from ancient Greek and means "the land between the rivers"). We know that they came from somewhere else, but we don't know precisely where that was. It seems likely that they arrived on ships, and they brought with them their own language that was unique and unlike any other language before or since.

Historians have speculated that the Sumerians came from present-day India, Africa, Iran, Caucasia, or even from Tibet. To date, we are not certain if any of these are correct. The Sumerians left behind vast numbers of cuneiform tablets on which characters were scratched while the clay was wet. While this writing (which also seems to have been the first form of complex writing ever) tells us a great deal about the Sumerians, it provides no clues as to where these people originated. Although they didn't seem to conquer the region by force of arms, they settled and gradually spread until their influence reached every part of Mesopotamia. Even their name is strange; the modern term Sumerian is derived from the name that these people used to describe themselves: *sang-ngiga*, meaning "black-heads."

Within three hundred years of their first arrival, these new people had built canals and ditches to create irrigation systems that made already fertile farming land even more productive. They also seemed to have used wheeled vehicles and small sailing vessels, two things that had not been seen before either in Mesopotamia or anywhere else. They established towns that gradually expanded to become the first cities, and the indigenous people were displaced, moving away from the land colonized by the Sumerians. Around 3000 BCE, the Sumerians began to do something that, up to this time, no one else had done on a large scale before: they began to smelt bronze.

Humans had been working metal long before the Sumerians arrived in Mesopotamia. Both copper and tin were used to make tools and other artifacts (some historians refer to the period immediately before the Bronze Age as the Copper Age). However, there is a fundamental problem with both copper and tin: both are relatively soft and malleable, and tools made from either tend to wear very quickly. While items made from these metals are acceptable for making decorative items such as jewelry, neither is good for producing hard-wearing tools or weapons. The Sumerians seem to have been the first to create an alloy (a substance made by mixing two or more metals). They added a little molten tin to a larger quantity of melted copper to produce bronze. Bronze is much harder than either copper or tin, and it does not wear in the same way, meaning that it can be used to cast objects such as tools and weapons, though it can also be used to make decorative items.

Before this time, people had used either crude stone tools or items made from copper. Making bronze tools suddenly opened new horizons for the Sumerians. With sharper, hard-wearing tools, they could undertake even more impressive excavations to improve irrigation systems and to make entirely new items such as looms to make some of the first woven fabrics and kilns in which to dry mud bricks. This produced a new building material that was stronger and more durable, which allowed the construction of larger buildings. As these were built, they merged to create the first cities. By around 3000 BCE, it is believed that there were up to twelve Sumerian cities in Mesopotamia, each with its own laws and each ruled by a hereditary priest-king. One of those cities, Uruk, is generally recognized as being the first true city in human history.

One notable thing is that neither copper nor tin was found naturally in quantity in Mesopotamia. Nor was there a great deal of wood (needed for the smelting process). To make bronze, the Sumerians had to import copper, tin, and wood. It seems that they created a lively trade network where they exchanged agricultural produce, woven fabrics, pottery, and later bronze artifacts for the raw materials they needed. The Sumerians also seem to have used sailing ships to obtain raw materials from further afield. Archeological evidence suggests that Sumerian traders may have visited many distant places in search of the resources they needed, including the Indus Valley in present-day Pakistan.

It is difficult to over-emphasize the significance of the Sumerians in terms of their overall contribution to human history. In the space of around 300 years, they brought technological and societal change at a rate that has rarely been equaled since. When they arrived in 3300 BCE, Mesopotamia had seen the beginnings of agriculture and the creation of the first settled human groups. The Sumerians brought incredibly rapid change that saw, within 300 years, bronze smelting, the production of bronze tools and weapons, and the creation of the first cities.

Some of their priests studied astronomy and created the very first calendar, something that was incredibly useful in planning the planting and harvest of crops. Sumerian astronomy appears to have been very sophisticated indeed, even compared to what followed. For example, one artifact called the Planisphere tablet was recovered during a dig in a Sumerian site. Archeologists had no idea of what the tablet meant. It was only with the advent of computer technology in the late twentieth century that it was realized that this was an astrolabe, a sophisticated star map that recorded the impact of a large asteroid in present-day Austria in 3123 BCE! How the Sumerians were able to observe and accurately record this event that took place far from their homelands remains a complete mystery.

This knowledge was supported by the first study of advanced mathematics, though the Sumerian system used a base of sixty rather than the base ten that is used today (which is why, even today, we have sixty seconds in a minute and sixty minutes in an hour). They also introduced, again for the first time as far as we know, the use of the wheel to create more effective plows and carts that could be used to transport agricultural produce further and more quickly.

We simply don't know if, for example, the use of the wheel and bronze smelting were already known to the Sumerians when they arrived in Mesopotamia or if these were things that were developed after they arrived. We also know that bronze tools and weapons didn't suddenly replace existing stone and copper implements. Bronze was simply better and stronger, and after its first introduction, bronze tools and weapons gradually replaced older versions.

What we can be certain of is that the trade routes established by the Sumerians helped to spread their knowledge throughout the region. Initially, their knowledge of bronze working would have made them invincible because it would have given them weapons and armor that no other people possessed. As this knowledge was passed to a wider area, the Bronze Age began to spread, and other people gained the new technology first developed by the Sumerians, as well as the use of writing, mathematics, and astronomy that they appear to have introduced.

Chapter Three

The Mediterranean

"I live again and again after death like Ra day by day."

—Egyptian Book of the Dead

Sumerian Mesopotamia seems to have endured for almost 1,000 years, though as a loose affiliation of city-states rather than as a single nation or empire. It would not be until the emergence of a new empire from the north, from a Semitic-speaking city-state known as Akkad, that it would finally be displaced. Even then, when all of Mesopotamia fell under the control of the Akkadian Empire, Sumerian writing and religion endured, and the scientific and technological advances introduced by the Sumerians continued to have a major impact.

The trade routes established by the Sumerian culture spread beyond the borders of Mesopotamia, particularly to other countries around the Mediterranean Sea. One notable example is Ancient Egypt, which at that time existed as a loose confederation of often warring states. From around the time that trade with Sumerian Mesopotamia began around 3150 BCE, bronze working began to appear in Egypt for the first time. Improved methods of agriculture also began to be used, including irrigation (at that time, the climate of Egypt was far less arid than it is today, and large areas of this region were very fertile). Egyptians also began to create their own form of writing using hieroglyphs (similar markings were used in the earliest Sumerian writing). They also used new building techniques that allowed the construction of larger and more durable buildings and cities. It seems certain that the knowledge that enabled these advances was imported from Sumerian Mesopotamia.

Thereafter, Egypt gradually became a single unified kingdom, with the Early Dynastic Period (3150-2686 BCE) followed by the creation of the Old Kingdom. These periods saw unprecedented advances in agriculture, building, and science and technology. It was during the Old Kingdom, while Sumerians still ruled in Mesopotamia, that the Giza Pyramids and the Sphinx were built. Just as in Mesopotamia, large cities were created in Egypt using kiln-dried bricks, and the whole of Egypt was ruled for the first time by a single administration overseen by a king.

In Egypt, perhaps even more than in Mesopotamia, we can see for the first time the rise of human societies that were quite different from what had come before but are remarkably similar to everything that would follow. Improved methods of agriculture and the widespread availability of bronze tools and implements led to abundant food during much of this time. Society became stratified and specialized. A class of hereditary nobles emerged, supported by priests (who also acted as proto-scientists) and a vast administration of civil servants who were responsible for the collection of taxes and the enforcement of laws. Artisans and craftsmen of every type emerged, and the products they made were bought and sold by growing numbers of merchants and traders. Underpinning all this activity was the bulk of the workforce, ordinary people who worked in the fields and in emerging industries.

Many of these people lived in cities constructed from bricks and spanning everything from areas of the poorest housing to opulent royal palaces, public areas, and places of worship. By around 2500 BCE, Egypt had eclipsed Mesopotamia in terms of wealth and power and had become one of the largest and most powerful nations in the world. Other nations in the region also embraced the new technology and new ideas flowing from Mesopotamia.

The Eutresis culture in present-day Greece (also known as the Early Helladic I culture) saw a gradual transition from mainly stone tools to bronze from around 3200 BCE to 2600 BCE. This period also saw the adoption of more effective forms of agriculture, which would lead to the emergence of a specific Greek culture that would endure until the end of the Bronze Age.

The rise of the Eutresis culture was paralleled by another in the same area, the Minoan. The Minoan civilization was centered on the Island of Crete and first began the transition from the use of stone to the use of bronze around 3100 BCE. This led to an explosion in new forms of art and monumental architecture and led to the Minoan culture dominating much of the surrounding region during the Bronze Age.

Sumerian influence extended beyond the shores of the Mediterranean. Elam was an ancient civilization located in present-day Iran and Iraq. Elam (this name is from a Sumerian word) seems to have had a close association with Sumerian culture in Mesopotamia and quickly adopted new technologies and new approaches to farming. From its capital at Susa in the Khuzestan lowlands, it developed a distinctive culture and would remain one of the most important sources of new developments throughout the Bronze Age.

The Bronze Age can be said to have originated in Sumerian Mesopotamia. However, the need for the Sumerians to import a constant supply of raw materials led to the creation of trade networks that spread new knowledge around the Mediterranean and beyond. Some of the cultures that subsequently emerged, including Egypt, would outlast and surpass the wealth and power of Sumerian Mesopotamia. And, of course, the Bronze Age wasn't confined to nations in close proximity to Mesopotamia.

Chapter Four

Central Asia and China

"Dripping water can penetrate the stone."

—Chinese proverb

The Bronze Age did not arrive in China until perhaps 1,000 years after it first began in Mesopotamia. A question that is still the subject of heated debate amongst historians is whether the Bronze Age arose spontaneously there or whether it was the result of contact with other civilizations in Central Asia that may have themselves traded with Mesopotamia.

The first archeologically confirmed dynasty to have ruled the Yellow River region of China was the Shang, which emerged in 1760 BCE and remained the dominant power in this area throughout the remainder of the Bronze Age. According to legend, the Shang was created when it overthrew an even earlier dynasty in the region, the Xia dynasty. No physical evidence has yet been found to confirm the existence of this earlier dynasty, and most of what we know of the Bronze Age history of China concerns the Shang dynasty.

Relatively recent archeological finds have produced bronze artifacts that seem to pre-date the Shang dynasty, but there is no general agreement on whether these were indigenously produced, independent of developments in the Mediterranean, or whether these might have been imported from elsewhere. What we do know with certainty is that during the Shang dynasty, metalworkers began to produce high-quality bronze that was used to make weapons and tools. Bronze swords and spearheads used by Shang troops would certainly have given them a notable advantage over other armies equipped with more primitive weapons.

Bronze working wasn't the only innovation introduced during this period. Shang armies incorporated wheeled chariots that allowed them to move rapidly and provided a platform from which archers equipped with composite bows could rain arrows on the enemy. These things certainly helped to make the Shang invincible in battle, but other developments in this period also parallel those that had taken place much earlier in Mesopotamia.

The first system of writing in China was developed, and it seems that some of the first Chinese cities also emerged. The walled city of Shang, located near the present-day city of Zhengzhou in Henan province, was the heart of this dynasty, and like the cities that had previously emerged in Mesopotamia and elsewhere, it seems to confirm the emergence of a new social hierarchy. The inner walls formed a safe refuge where palaces and places of worship were located. This area also seems to have included facilities for the smelting of brass, suggesting that this emerging technology was a closely guarded secret, probably undertaken by artisans of the highest skills. Other industries and crafts were undertaken outside this central area but protected by a second wall. The outer area also seems to have included housing for workers and artisans who were not involved directly in the production of brass artifacts. The territory ruled by the Shang dynasty included a number of other walled cities, all laid out in a similar way.

There are close parallels between the changes that took place in China during the Shang dynasty and those that had taken place in Mesopotamia, Egypt, and other areas about

1,000 years before. There was very limited trade between China and the West during this period (the Silk Road, the network of Eurasian trade routes, did not yet exist during the Bronze Age). We simply do not know whether the emergence of bronze working during the Shang dynasty was the result of a transfer of new technologies and ideas from the West or an autonomous and indigenous development.

It is certainly notable that many cultures in Central Asia—the bridge between China and the West, including the steppes of Russia and Kazakhstan as well as regions of present-day Afghanistan, Kyrgyzstan, Uzbekistan, Tajikistan, and Turkmenistan—seemed to move into the Bronze Age before China. We know that there was at least some limited trade between Eurasia and China during this period, so it is certainly possible that China learned of bronze working through Eurasia.

One of the problems with providing dates for the Bronze Age is that this wasn't something that happened all over the world at the same time. Instead, it appears to have spread out from its origin in Mesopotamia like ripples in a pond, reaching nations in the area quickly but taking much longer to reach more distant lands. That was true not just of places as far from the epicenter as China but also in areas geographically much closer to the Fertile Crescent. Recent archeological findings have even cast doubt on this theory, suggesting perhaps that bronze working emerged in other areas independent of Mesopotamia and, in some cases, well before that area became the home to the Sumerians!

Chapter Five

Central and Western Europe

"History, after all, is a process, not a position, and it is not best written in bronze and marble."

—David Olusoga

Tracing the spread of the Bronze Age in Europe is very difficult, mainly because it was intermittent and uneven in its distribution. Relatively recent archeological findings in the Balkans have even discovered bronze artifacts that appear to pre-date Sumerian bronze working in Mesopotamia, raising the possibility that the smelting of bronze in this area may have developed independently.

A report published in 2013 on excavations in archeological sites in present-day Serbia and Bulgaria included some surprising results. One dig in particular, at a Neolithic village site near the town of Pločnik, included the discovery of the remains of what appeared to be a copper workshop including a furnace and a few copper tools. These were dated to 5500 BCE, well before copper was generally thought to have been worked in this area. The excavation also discovered a small bronze foil dated to around 4600 BCE—over 1,500 years before the Sumerians began smelting bronze in Mesopotamia. This certainly seems to prove that an understanding of bronze smelting existed well before 3300 BCE, the date usually given for the beginning of the Bronze Age.

Subsequent discoveries in Serbia and Bulgaria produced more bronze artifacts that were all dated to before 4000 BCE. However, these artifacts are rare, and they do not seem to indicate the widespread use of bronze to produce tools and weapons. There also seems to be a large gap between these very early bronze artifacts in the Balkans and the widespread use of bronze tools that emerged over 1,000 years later. It seems that bronze working was developed in this area well before the Bronze Age, lasted for around 500 years, and then, for unknown reasons, disappeared. Just like so many aspects of the Bronze Age, these new discoveries have not yet been explained, and we await further excavations to produce additional evidence.

Other finds in Central Europe seem to follow a more conventional chronology. For example, digs in the Czech Republic have revealed the existence of a Bronze Age culture in that area, the Únětice. Other findings that seem to originate from the same culture have been discovered in different areas, including Germany, Austria, Slovakia, Poland, and even as far east as Ukraine. This culture seems to have emerged around 2300 BCE and incorporated the widespread use of bronze for the manufacture of tools and weapons. The timing suggests that this may have been due to the spread of knowledge from Mesopotamia. We know very little about this widespread Bronze Age culture, but it is notable that some burial sites included gold artifacts. This suggests the burial of important people, which in turn points to a stratification of society that may mirror that seen in Mesopotamia and other cultures adjacent to the Mediterranean Sea.

The manufacture of bronze items appears to have spread to northern Europe, and some very impressive bronze items have been found at sites in northern Germany. In Britain too, the arrival of the Bronze Age seems to have followed a familiar pattern of a gradual spread of knowledge. It has proved very difficult to establish the precise beginning of the Bronze Age in Britain, with estimates ranging from 2500 BCE to 2000 BCE. The primary culture at this time has been identified as the Bell Beaker culture, named after a distinctive style of pottery that emerged at this time.

The Bell Beaker culture was responsible for the creation of some of the largest megalithic monuments in Britain (including Seahenge, Silbury Hill, and the latter phases of Stonehenge). Recent discoveries suggest that this may have been a culture that reached the British Isles from elsewhere. Scientific analysis of human remains from this period has revealed that some seem to have originated in present-day Switzerland. This raises the intriguing possibility that what took place in Britain followed the pattern established in Mesopotamia, with incomers who possessed advanced technology and knowledge gradually supplanting the existing culture.

Other theories suggest that the people who became the Bell Beaker culture may have originated in the Iberian Peninsula, the Netherlands, or Central Europe. Wherever they came from, these people brought with them metal working, first using copper and then, from around 2150 BCE, bronze.

It certainly seems to be true that the completion of some of the most impressive megalithic sites that had been started by the previous indigenous culture took place after the arrival of these incomers. The workforce required for these projects, as well as the discovery of high-status burial sites for individuals, seems to suggest that in Britain, as elsewhere during the Bronze Age, societies became more hierarchical, with a clear distinction between nobles and the mass of ordinary people.

Just as the Bronze Age arrived in Britain later than in other areas, it ended later too. Although the end of the Bronze Age is generally taken to be around 1200 BCE, the beginning of the Iron Age in Britain did not begin until as late as 600 BCE. Because Britain is one of the most isolated parts of Europe and one of the furthest from Mesopotamia, this seems to reinforce the theory of a gradual spread of knowledge across the continent from its origins in the Middle East.

Chapter Six

The Nordic Bronze Age

"People at that time often traveled far, especially the women."

—Kristian Kristiansen

The Bronze Age reached the Nordic countries (present-day Denmark, Finland, Norway, and Sweden) in the extreme north of Europe later than in any other region, with the earliest indigenous bronze artifacts being dated to around 1700 BCE, over 1,000 years after the production of bronze tools and weapons had become common in other areas. Partly, this seems to have been a function of the distance of this region from the epicenter of the Bronze Age, but also due to a scarcity of raw materials; neither copper nor tin are to be found in appreciable quantities in this region.

The only way for bronze to reach the Nordic countries was by importing both bronze itself and the copper and tin needed to produce it. Artifacts found in the Nordic countries have been found to use bronze that originated in Mycenaean Greece, a distance of over 2,000 miles (3,000 kilometers). Perhaps nothing better illustrates the trade network that spanned Europe and the Middle East in the Bronze Age than the fact that it was possible to transport bronze over such vast distances.

Just as in other areas, the introduction of bronze working was accompanied by developments that brought other societal changes to the Nordic countries. Improved methods of agriculture and new building materials meant that people tended to live in settled communities that evolved into towns and cities. Food surpluses meant that artisans and merchants became important, especially in the Nordic countries where so many raw materials had to be imported. People emerged for the first time who had some control over the distribution of food and resources, and this meant the acquisition of wealth and power by a few.

In the Nordic countries (as also seen, for example, in the British Isles), burial practices in the Stone Age were often based on communal burial sites. During the Bronze Age, memorial burial sites for individuals or families became more common, and often these sites included valuable artifacts that would have belonged to those buried there during life.

The Bronze Age in the Nordic countries also marks the beginning of the warrior caste for which this area would become famous. A great many of the most intricately worked pieces of bronze work that have been discovered in this region are not decorative items but weapons, helmets, and armor. The Nordic Bronze Age was also the period during which the first large-scale battles seem to have taken place. It seems very likely that the new elites that the Bronze Age produced protected themselves and their power and wealth by acquiring and arming followers. These soon became the first armies, and it doesn't appear to have taken long for these to be used not just for protection but to expand the power and reach of one group by attacking another.

Before the Bronze Age, large-scale battles were unknown, or at least no evidence of such conflicts has been found. There almost certainly were conflicts, but these would most likely have involved no more than a couple of dozen people from rival tribal groups of hunter-gatherers armed with primitive stone weapons. The Bronze Age brought not just more lethal weapons and more effective armor but also the emergence of warriors who specialized in fighting. Nowhere is that more evident than in the Nordic countries, where the warrior ethos became fused with religion to elevate prowess in combat to a mystical level. The heroes and gods that would become a mainstay of Norse religion almost certainly first emerged at this time, and these characters were almost always characterized not by wisdom or a willingness to govern peacefully but by crafty strategy and ability to wield the new weapons in the most effective way.

It is interesting to note that when the Bronze Age finally began in the Nordic countries, it was less than 500 years from ending in other areas and being replaced by the Iron Age. Just like the British Isles, the Nordic countries were late to enter the Bronze Age and late to move into the next age.

Chapter Seven

International Trade and Globalization

"It was a period of globalization, or at least interconnection, not rivaled again until the modern day."

—Professor Eric H. Cline

One of the most notable aspects of the Bronze Age was the expansion of global trade. In part, this was driven directly by the need to create bronze. In Mesopotamia, where the Bronze Age began, there was almost no copper or tin and relatively little wood, which was needed to power the furnaces used to smelt bronze. The Sumerians were forced to seek these raw materials elsewhere. They established trade routes that exchanged the surplus food that their advanced agriculture made possible, as well as pottery and fabric, for the copper, tin, and wood they needed. Very few areas of the world provided abundant resources of copper, tin, and timber, so virtually every subsequent region that adopted bronze working was also forced to establish new trade routes. This led to the creation of a network of global trade that was astounding in its scope and reach, and that has only been equaled in relatively recent history.

Areas that were rich in these resources became centers of trade. The Island of Cyprus in the Mediterranean, for example, was rich in copper, while the southeast of present-day Britain and parts of present-day Afghanistan were the locations of a number of productive tin mines. Gradually, a trade network developed between these areas and the growing Bronze Age powers: Sumerian Mesopotamia, Egypt, and the Akkadian Empire. The heart of this network stretched from Italy in the east to Afghanistan in the west and from Turkey in the north to Egypt in the south, though trade extended well beyond this core area. This led to something completely new—a worldwide trading system that focused on metal, mainly tin and copper but also gold, as well as precious and semi-precious stones that, for the first time, gained intrinsic economic value.

But it wasn't just commodities that were exchanged. People involved in trade took ideas with them, and specialist artisans could find lucrative employment in distant areas that lacked their skills. Ancient records inscribed on clay tablets and discovered by archeologists provide a rich source of data. These describe kings exchanging gifts of precious commodities and of people: artisans, musicians, artists, and writers might find themselves sent to a foreign land or might themselves choose to move to an area where they could easily find employment for a local ruler.

This vast trade network spread out from the Mediterranean across much of Eurasia. A number of archeological finds in Greece have provided several notable examples. It seems that Greece was an exporter of agricultural surpluses, including olives, honey, cheeses, wines, and pulses. Greek cultures, particularly the Mycenaean, were also famous during the Bronze Age for the quality of the pottery they produced. This distinctive pottery has been found at many sites, including on the Atlantic coast of Europe, on the Baltic Sea, and in present-day Turkey.

Conversely, Greece was also an importer of many things, including metals, wood, pepper, fish, and slaves. Archeological findings in the Aegean have discovered items that originated in Egypt, Turkey, Cyprus, Mesopotamia, and many other areas. It would appear that by the Late Bronze Age, the Greek economy had become heavily dependent on both imports and exports. The same thing is true of most of the other developed regions in the world at this time. It appears that the vast majority of this trade was carried out by private merchants, many of whom became immensely wealthy as a result. Kingdoms rarely seem to have become directly involved in trade, with the exception of essential foods including grain, where prices were sometimes fixed in order to ensure that bread was freely available and affordable for ordinary people.

Interconnectedness is a term that gained popularity in the late twentieth century to describe international trade and communication. The truth seems to be that the Bronze Age world was also deeply interconnected, with the economies of many regions becoming wholly dependent on their ability to import and export. Archeological evidence suggests that the network of international trade that emerged during the Bronze Age was just as complex as the trade networks that were established in the nineteenth and twentieth centuries.

The only significant difference between trade during the Bronze Age and more recent times was the means of transporting goods. Goods moved via overland routes would have been carried by pack animals or in horse-drawn carts. Roads in the modern sense generally did not exist, and traders would have used tracks that were probably unusable during bad weather. At sea and particularly in the Mediterranean and Aegean Seas, small sailing ships were used to convey cargo. These sea routes would have included the Greek mainland and islands, Egypt, Turkey, Cyprus, Crete, and locations in the Central and Eastern Mediterranean. However, even during the early Bronze Age, longer voyages were undertaken by merchants using sailing ships. Evidence has been found in Sumerian sites in Mesopotamia that indicate imports of, for example, carnelian (a semi-precious stone) both from the Indus Valley in present-day Pakistan and from Gujarat in present-day India.

Connectivity was an essential and often overlooked aspect of the Bronze Age. People became used to (and in some cases dependent on) the import of raw materials, food, and other commodities from far-distant regions. The economies of many regions also became heavily reliant on the export of certain goods, either to exchange these for imports or as a source of revenue. This connectivity also led to the widespread movement of people who took with them new ideas, new technologies, and new cultural approaches. It was this interconnectivity that gave many Bronze Age civilizations their richness through exposure to the influence of distant cultures. But any such system must also be fragile. The economies of many, many regions became utterly dependent on international trade and communication, and when this eventually failed, they suffered an abrupt decline.

Chapter Eight

Life in the Bronze Age

"Stone Age. Bronze Age. Iron Age. We define entire epics of humanity by the technology they use."

—Reed Hastings

As you will now appreciate, there wasn't a single Bronze Age culture or society. Different places were at different stages in development, and for the first time, indigenous cultures were exposed to artifacts and ideas from distant lands. In some locations, incomers brought an entirely new way of life that replaced what had come before. New societal divisions meant that rulers, nobles, wealthy merchants, and senior priests at one end of the societal scale and the slaves who underpinned virtually every Bronze Age culture at the opposite end of that scale lived extraordinary lives. But what was the Bronze Age like for the vast majority of ordinary people? There is no single answer, but let's look at two specific areas—the British Isles on the periphery of Europe and Greece, close to the heart of the Bronze Age—to try to gain an understanding of everyday life in this fascinating period.

The people who inhabited the British Isles during the Bronze Age left very few written records, so what we know about their lives must be inferred from archeological finds. Britain during the Bronze Age was still largely covered in forest, making overland travel difficult and dangerous. Most long-distance transportation relied on rivers, typically utilizing log boats propelled by oars. It wouldn't be until late in the Bronze Age that the first wheeled carts arrived in Britain, and up to that time, people traveled on foot or, for the wealthy few, on horseback.

There were no cities to compare with those emerging around the Mediterranean. Towns tended to be small, with a handful of round, thatch-roofed houses, usually surrounded by a wooden wall to keep domestic animals (mainly sheep but also pigs and cattle) inside and to provide protection from wolves and other predators from the outside. Domesticated dogs were present too, to help guard domestic animals. The men of the town hunted boar and deer in the forests, probably accompanied and assisted by dogs. Fish were caught in nearby rivers, and crops including wheat, peas, and beans were grown in fields close to towns.

The people wore clothing made from flax linen and used clay cups and cooking pots. They had many bronze items, including tools, farming implements, and even a few simple weapons such as daggers. Food seems to have been abundant and varied through a combination of hunting, gathering wild nuts, berries, and honey, and through simple agriculture. Compared to many other Bronze Age societies, life in Britain was relatively primitive, but surprisingly, even here the interconnectivity of the world was apparent. In an archeological excavation of a Bronze Age settlement near the River Nene in England, amber beads were discovered that must have originated in present-day Iran, thousands of miles away!

Life in cities during the Bronze Age was very different, though even in the most advanced areas, these were relatively small compared to those that would follow. Even in Mesopotamian Sumer, none had more than 100,000 occupants, and most were much smaller. This was mainly a matter of simple logistics. City dwellers generally don't produce their own food. The food they consume must be brought in from outside, partly through imports from other areas but mainly from nearby farms. Agriculture and transport advanced greatly during the Bronze Age, but neither were able to sustain very large urban populations. Water was also a problem. Cities provided communal wells for the use of their inhabitants, but there was a limit to how many people could be kept supplied with water.

Excavations of the remains of a number of Bronze Age cities, mainly in Greece and around the Mediterranean, imply that people lived in multi-room houses constructed from bricks and often arranged around a central courtyard. Extended families lived within these houses, and they also often included burial plots in the courtyard. In most cities, there was no form of urban planning, and housing grew in a haphazard way, leading to narrow, winding, and probably congested streets. Few cities provided effective drainage or sanitation systems, and disease was a constant threat for city dwellers, particularly if limited water supplies became contaminated by human waste.

Most cities included a stratified society. In Babylon, for example, which became the largest city in Mesopotamia, clay tablets tell us that there were three distinct classes of people: hereditary nobles (including the king), free men, and slaves. Only the hereditary nobility could occupy the highest position as advisers to the king, the most senior priestly positions, and senior ranks in the army. Free men were able to follow a range of professions, including artisans working with metals, ceramics, and fabrics, builders, and as ship and cart builders. There were also merchants, though despite many becoming extremely wealthy, this was not a highly regarded way of life in the Bronze Age. There was also a new professional class that included lawyers (some of the first codes of law were created in the cities of the Bronze Age), doctors, and even (generally within the priesthood) what we would now call scientists, those who studied the natural world. In some cities, residents had access to places of entertainment where they would be exposed to the talents of musicians, actors, and performers, many of whom came from other areas.

Just as in Britain, connectivity was an important factor for these city dwellers. The slaves that they owned often originated from distant places (Egypt was a major source of slaves throughout the Bronze Age), some of the food that they ate and the wine that they drank was imported, and many of the practical and decorative items in their homes came from far away or was made locally but using imported raw materials.

Whether they lived in relatively primitive Britain or in one of the great urban centers of Mesopotamia, there were certain changes that the Bronze Age brought to virtually every person in Eurasia and beyond. The daily struggle to find enough food that had characterized the Stone Age had largely disappeared, partly through the availability of improved tools and weapons and partly through the increasing use of settled agriculture and the raising of domestic animals. The emergence of a more stratified society meant that most people found themselves under the control of some form of ruler.

The most single significant factor was that few Bronze Age cultures were self-sufficient. All relied to a greater or lesser extent on contact and trade with other cultures, but this would prove to be fragile and one of the fundamental causes of its sudden collapse.

Chapter Nine

The Abrupt End of the Bronze Age

"A catastrophic end of an epoch, in which many of the great empires were blown away in a storm of destruction."

—Gordon Doherty

The Bronze Age represents a period of rapid and fundamental change in human culture and society that has not been seen before or since. Those changes relied on the ability of disparate cultures to trade with one another—to import the raw materials they needed and to export their own products and surplus food. For over 1,500 years, this system worked. And then, abruptly, it didn't. Just as the origin of the Bronze Age involved a mysterious people, the Sumerians, its abrupt end involved another people about who we know virtually nothing—the Sea People.

That term is a recent one used by historians. At the time, the cultures of Greece, Egypt, Mesopotamia, and Cyprus gave them a range of different names. The one thing that all agreed on was that these marauding, warlike people came from somewhere else, and they brought with them chaos and ruin. No historical investigation has revealed a point of origin for these people, and they appear to have left no written records that help to illuminate their own history. They may have originated somewhere in the Mediterranean, or the Aegean, or perhaps even in Anatolia (Turkey).

Egyptian records tell us that the Sea People first appeared in present-day Syria before moving through present-day Lebanon and Israel before arriving in Egypt itself. From there, they spread out to conquer other kingdoms. Many cultures produced artwork that claimed to show these fearsome invaders, but these tell us little. Some show them as wearing feathered headdresses, rather like those of Native American tribes. Others appear to show them as bearded barbarians wearing horned helmets. Some show them as looking very like the armies of the nations that they attacked. The one thing that all accounts agree on is that these people were armed with bronze weapons and were adept in the use of war chariots.

The Egyptian accounts give the year 1177 BCE as the beginning of the attack by waves of invaders by land and sea. Egypt itself survived, but Mycenaean Greece, the empire of the Hittites, and the Island of Cyprus were conquered. The invaders fought with ferocity and almost unbroken success on land and at sea. Nowhere was safe, and the interconnected world was shattered completely and in a stunningly short period of time.

Those areas that were not directly attacked found themselves cut off from the imports and exports that had become critical. Within one century, almost all the great civilizations of the Bronze Age were reduced to ruins or to a shadow of their former power. For a very long time, historians believed that the arrival of the Sea People brought about the end of the Bronze Age, but more recent investigations have suggested that although they were certainly a factor, this huge change wasn't just due to human incursion but also to climate change and natural disasters.

As recently as 2014, researchers analyzing core samples taken from the area of the Sea of Galilee discovered that, from around 1250 to 1100 BCE, this area experienced a 150-year-long "megadrought." In some areas, this catastrophic drought may have lasted up to 300 years, almost certainly meaning widespread crop failures and famine. Some civilizations—those in Egypt and some city-states in Mesopotamia for example—were spared the worst impact of the drought because of the proximity of much of their farming land to large rivers, but for most people in the region, once-productive farming land was transformed into arid desert which would have led to desperate food shortages. A few of the surviving writings from the Late Bronze Age are messages from one king to another calling urgently for additional shipments of food.

A disastrous drought and the famine it brought was a huge problem for the people who had been at the very heart of the Bronze Age, but there was another major issue. In the 50-year period from 1225 to 1175 BCE in the eastern Mediterranean and Aegean, there was what has been called an "earthquake storm." This is a sequence of earthquakes where the first earthquake causes additional stress on the next part of a fault line and that, days, weeks, or even years later, causes another earthquake on the same fault. Recent investigation has shown that many of the principal cities of the Late Bronze Age in this region were built on or close to fault lines. Each of these earthquakes that took place would have been sufficiently powerful to destroy buildings and perhaps whole cities.

It is a possibility that the Sea People themselves may have been impelled to leave their homelands, wherever they were, by a combination of drought and famine. Individually, it seems unlikely that either drought, earthquakes, or an invasion could have brought the Bronze Age to an end. The combination of all three occurring at approximately the same time presented what has been called a "perfect storm of calamities." This was made worse by the very interconnectedness that had helped the Bronze Age to spread.

Cultures had become utterly dependent on both imports and exports. Famine would have made it difficult to import food, and the marauding Sea People would have made all trade routes, on land and at sea, hazardous and unreliable. Cut off from the essential sources of food and raw materials on which they had come to depend, many of the most advanced and prosperous cultures in the eastern Mediterranean and the Aegean collapsed in a shockingly short space of time, and many of the most populated cities seem to have been abandoned.

The Bronze Age brought with it prosperity, abundant food, and a vast trade network. Its abrupt end around 1200 BCE plunged parts of Eurasia into a period of famine and shortage that, in some areas, would take hundreds of years to recover from.

Chapter Ten

After the Bronze Age

"By slow degrees the iron sword came to the fore; the bronze sickle fell into disrepute; the ploughman began to cleave the earth with iron."

—Lucretius

During the Late Bronze Age, major kingdoms in Mesopotamia, Anatolia, Greece, Egypt, and elsewhere formed a trading network that was more comprehensive and extensive than anything seen before. When any one of these civilizations collapsed, that inevitably placed more strain on the others until that collapse became general. Some of these civilizations vanished completely, including the Mycenaean Greeks, Minoans, and Hittites. Others, such as Egypt and the Assyrian Empire, seem to have endured through becoming virtually self-sufficient and no longer reliant on imports.

Whole schemes of knowledge were lost. Writing, for example, virtually ended in Greece and would not return for almost 300 years until the arrival of the Phoenicians, who brought with them a new alphabet. For this reason, the period following the collapse of the Bronze Age has been called a dark age, when the lack of written records means that we just don't know what took place in many areas.

The manufacture of bronze tools and weapons also effectively ended with the collapse of the Bronze Age. Few areas had access to the tin, copper, and wood needed to smelt bronze, and with the collapse of international trade, it became impossible to continue to make bronze items. People still needed metal tools and weapons, and the lack of the raw materials necessary to make bronze led to a search for a new metal that would not be dependent on the sourcing of raw materials from distant lands. That search would lead to the next great age in human history, where iron became the most commonly used metal.

Iron had been in use since around 2000 BCE, but it was seen as inferior to bronze and appears to have been little used. Driven by necessity, after the Bronze Age collapse, metalworkers began to experiment with making harder and more durable metal from iron ore and bog iron, both of which were present in many areas. It is difficult to be certain where this new use of iron began, though some accounts suggest that the metal workers on the Island of Cyprus may have been among the first to experiment with the manufacture of durable iron items as early as 1200 BCE, soon after the manufacture of bronze became impossible.

The subsequent history of humankind would be dominated (as in some ways it still is) by the manufacture of first iron and then steel to make new items that were even more durable and effective than those made from bronze. The Iron Age was not a logical progression from the Bronze Age but an entirely new approach forced on cultures by the collapse of the trade networks needed to produce bronze.

Conclusion

The Bronze Age was truly a defining period in human history. In fact, there have been few periods in the history of human culture and society that brought such rapid and far-reaching change. Many of the elements that we take for granted as part of everyday life in the twenty-first century—agriculture, writing, urban living, global trade networks, hierarchical and stratified societies, and the advancement of science and technology through the work of specialists—began in this period. Many of these things were made possible by the development of durable and effective bronze tools.

But the manufacture of bronze was the subject of one fundamental drawback: it was only possible as long as the necessary raw materials were available, which often meant importing them from distant lands. Beginning with the ancient Sumerians in Mesopotamia, it was this need that drove the establishment of extensive trade networks. The result was the emergence of a number of cultures based on the production of bronze; each became dependent on the others for imports and exports. For over a thousand years, that system continued without pause. Then came climate change, a storm of earthquakes, and the arrival of violent outsiders. The network that connected Bronze Age cultures had allowed the spread of knowledge and the transfer of goods. By the time of the Sea People and other disasters around 1200 BCE, that network had become essential to the viability of many of the most significant cultures. When it collapsed, they did too.

The end of the Bronze Age would lead to a new age, the Iron Age, where cultures were less reliant on trade with others. But the immediate aftermath of the Bronze Age brought a period of chaos and a loss of knowledge, some of which has not been regained even today. For example, we still do not know just how Sumerian astronomers were able to observe and record events such as the descent of an asteroid in 3123 BCE.

The Bronze Age continues to be beset by mysteries, partly because of the abrupt collapse of so many cultures when it ended. We still don't know where the Sumerians, the people who are generally credited with beginning the Bronze Age, came from. Nor do we know where the warlike Sea People, who contributed to its final collapse, originated. All that we can be truly certain of is that the period known as the Bronze

Age changed the way that people lived and interacted fundamentally and forever.

Bibliography

Anthony, D. W. (2007). *The Horse, the Wheel, and Language: How Bronze-Age Riders from the Eurasian Steppes Shaped the Modern World.*

Cline, E. H. (2014). *1177 B.C.: The Year Civilization Collapsed.*

Drews, R. (1993). *The End of the Bronze Age: Changes in Warfare and the Catastrophe ca. 1200 B.C.*

Scott, J. C. (2017). *Against the Grain: A Deep History of the Earliest States.*

Printed in Great Britain
by Amazon